For as in one body we have many members, and the members do not all have the same function, so we, though many, are one body in Christ, and individually members one of another.
--Romans 12:4-5 ESV

JOURNEY TO SPRITUAL FITNESS

BECOMING TEMPLE-FIT
MIND * BODY * HEART* SOUL * SPIRIT

Camielle L. Moore

Journey to Spiritual Fitness is a book and journal on being spiritually fit. The scriptures used in this book are not the property of the author. The author does not claim scriptures as creative property. Scriptures are used to support the readers of this book as they correlate life issues to the Word of God.

Cover Illustration Copyright © 2016 by Camielle L. Moore
Cover design by Tara L. Crumbie
Publishing and Editing by Camielle L. Moore
Author photograph by Camielle L. Moore

ISBN: 978-0-692-78832-5

CONTENTS

Introduction

INTRODUCTION

When God first gave me the title for this book, I was stunned. I didn't know why, and I certainly didn't know how in the world I was going to tell someone else how to get 'temple' and 'spiritually' fit when I was a mess myself! I had just had a major surgery, my dad passed away, and my mother was diagnosed with dementia. I was depressed, gaining weight, my recuperation from my surgery was going slower than anticipated—in other words, my temple was not very fit at all…in any area! But if I didn't know anything else I knew that I had to be obedient to what God had told me to do.

You see, I have known since I was six years old that God had called me to lead a ministry. For most of my life I ran from that calling because I thought He was calling me to preach. But it wasn't until September of 2011 did I stop running. I had just quit a terrible job, I was unhappy, depressed and feeling more lost than I ever had in my entire life. I remember sitting on my son's front porch in San Clemente, CA, and asking God what was it I was doing wrong?? Why was I so unhappy?? Why do I keep falling into depression and hopelessness?? And as clear as if He were sitting right next to me, that still small voice told me, 'Stop running from Me. It's time.' I just hung my head and cried because I knew exactly what He was talking about.

It would take another two years for me to realize I wasn't supposed to preach; I was supposed to minister to others with my life testimonies. So immediately I think 'Oh great! I'm going to have to go to school to be a Biblical counselor.'....blah, blah, blah and sigh! I started praying to God to show me what tools and schooling I would need to help me get started. And sure enough He did. I googled Christian counseling one day and the search turned up a place where I could work towards a certificate. However, they also had a program for Christian Life Coaching and let me tell you lightbulbs and bells started going off! Just as John the Baptist leaped in his mother Elizabeth's womb when Mary, Mother of Jesus, came to visit her, my *spirit* did the same! I had finally found what He wanted me to focus on. I was doing a hallelujah dance and praising God in our dining room! And as they say, 'the rest is history'.

As I was taking my courses, the Holy Spirit gave me the name 'Temple-Fit' for the ministry God wanted me to lead. And here I am! Ready to share my journey and experiences to show others how to become temple-fit, and Christian-fit in every part and aspect of their life.

Come, take a journey with me that will renew and restore your entire God-given temple. And, I pray and hope, that sharing my experiences in this book helps at least one person on their journey to becoming mind, body, heart, soul and spirit fit...Temple-Fit. God Bless You.

CHAPTER 1

TEMPLE YOU!

YOU! Yes YOU! Did you know that you are a temple? And not just any temple; you are the most amazing and beautiful temple on the face of the earth. Not the Taj Mahal, not the Temple of Heaven, nor St. Peter's Basilica. None of these temples compare to you!

You have been created in God's image, by His hand…not the hand of man, not by a machine, or in a factory. God took the time to form you; to mold you perfectly. You are a fearfully and wonderfully made temple of God. But what exactly does it mean when I tell you that?? Well, in the Hebrew text of the Bible, the word *fearfully* means, 'with great reverence, heart-felt interest and with respect.'; and the word *wonderfully* means, 'unique, set apart, marvelous'. Each strand of hair, each ear, each eye, each hand; every single part of you was carefully and lovingly designed to create the unique and one of a kind temple called YOU!

I am forever amazed at how every part of our temple—mind, body, heart, soul, and spirit—work together to keep us 'spiritually' fit. Each part has a role in maintaining the temple we dwell in. Each part speaks to each other. Each part feeds and nourishes the other parts so that they are able to work together to allow our temples to heal, to grow, to prosper, to rebuild, renew, and restore, just the way God intended. One of my favorite scriptures, Romans 12:4-5(ESV) says just this very thing, "For as in one body we have many members, and the members do not all have the same function, so we, though many, are one body in Christ, and individually members one of another." I believe that this applies to the parts of our God-given temple as well.

So many times we tend to forget just how amazingly made we truly are! If we take the world's word, we are never good enough just the way we are. The world tells young girls that they have to be practically a size 0, or 'hollywood skinny', to look attractive. The world tells young men, they have to have tons of muscles, not have a potbelly, or be over six feet tall to be attractive to anyone. These false dictations are just wrong and are not of God in any way!

God's Word tells us in Romans 12:2(NLT), "Do not conform to the pattern of this world,..." Falling for the worlds perception of who and what you should be like can and will wreak havoc in your Godly temple. It can cause depression, eating disorders, destructive behaviors and habits, low self-esteem issues, thoughts of suicide, and unfortunately actual suicide.

Deciding to not allow society to dictate who you are is a big step. And honestly, most people are afraid to disagree or not conform to the 'ways of the world'. Myself include. I spent years trying to be who society, friends, and family said I should. I was in my mid-twenties when I decided enough was a enough! I am ME! I am fearfully and wonderfully made because God broke the mold when He created me. I am unique, and I am a child of the most High God! And more importantly, because God says so! Making that decision and those declarations was the easy part. Learning to accept, love me, and live those declarations was the hard pat.

Can I be totally transparent with you? For most of my life I had felt less than who God says I am...fearfully and wonderfully made. I was that girl who wanted to look, be, and act like the popular girls; or the prettier girls ...even the girls in my own family. I was that girl who thought that I would be happiest, and more accepted, if I could just make others happy...no matter the cost to me. I wore makeup, hair extensions, dressed provocatively, got my nails done, held my tongue, and never spoke up for myself...all to please others in order to be liked and loved. But no matter what I did to 'fit' in, it never seemed to be enough. I found myself in toxic relationships with men, family, co-workers, and so-called friends. I was abused, used, and taken for granted in every way imaginable. And yet, I still I continued to accept it all, thinking it the norm and price I had to pay to be liked and loved. I was truly convinced I needed the approval of both those around me, and the world. All of this lead me to be depressed, unhappy, impacted how I raised my children, and yes, thoughts of and an attempt at suicide.

But for God, I would probably still be stuck in that miserable and toxic cycle, living with an unfit temple. Because you see it wasn't just my mind that was unfit because it was conforming to the world's view, but also my body—because I answered to my fleshly desires, was in physically abusive relationships, I drank, I didn't rest or eat the way that I should; in my heart because I made decisions and went into toxic and abusive relationships based on my feelings; my soul because I never had any peace; and my spirit because I had no will, or idea on how to get out of the vicious cycle I was in.

It is imperative to remember for that as fearfully, wonderfully, and uniquely made that we are, this temple is not ours. The last part of 1Corinthians 6:19(NIV) tells us this very thing, "...You are not your own;" Yet, we sometimes treat our mind, body, heart, soul, and spirit with disrespect, lack of care, and lack of love. We allow people, alcohol, drugs, physical and mental abuse, and negative thoughts, environments, and words to damage our one-of-a-kind temple. We forget what a price was paid on our behalf for this temple, and 1Corinthians 6:20(KJV) reminds us that, "For ye are bought with a price: therefore glorify God in your body, and in your spirit, which are God's." If we wish to have a temple that is fit and truly honors God, we must remind ourselves 'whose' we are!

Learning to love God and trust His love and His Word about who *you* are, and *whose* you are, will help you to begin to let go of the shackles and false perceptions of the world, eventually causing you to fall in love with yourself...God's way. Learning to love yourself completely, and accepting who YOU are is crucial to becoming temple fit. Just like all parts of the 'body of Christ' have to work together for that body to work, all parts of your temple— mind, body, heart, soul, and spirit—have to also work together to make you fit and able to live God's purpose, and the passion He has given you for your life.

God is love, and if you are of God and fearfully and wonderfully made in His image, then that means that you are love as well. And since God loves you completely and unconditionally, you need to learn to see yourself through His eyes and love yourself completely and unconditionally as well. Also, remember to do as Psalm 139:14 says and 'praise' God that you are fearfully and wonderfully made. Once you do these things you will be on your way to freeing each part of your temple from all of the things that have been holding it captive.

STUDY SCRIPTURES

- Romans 12:4-5
- Romans 12:2
- 1 Corinthians 6:19 & 20
- Psalm 139:14

JOURNALING QUESTIONS

1. What things about your temple show and remind you just how fearfully and wonderfully made?

_____

_____

_____

_____

2. In what ways do you give God praise for how fearfully and wonderfully made you are?

_____

_____

_____

_____

3. What makes your God-given temple unique?

_____

_____

_____

_____

4. What part, or parts, of your temple contribute to you not being 'temple-fit'? Why?

_____

_____

_____

_____

5. Which scripture, or scriptures, from this chapter spoke to your current state of temple-fitness? Why?

_____

_____

_____

_____

CHAPTER 2

JOURNEY LEG: MIND-FIT

Okay, so now you know that YOU are a temple, one of the most magnificent, beautiful temples ever created. You know that to love God is to love yourself. Well now let's continue our journey by learning about become mind-fit.

Nowadays, most people are really into 'detoxing' their bodies; but what about detoxing our minds?? We detox impurities from our bodies by doing cleanses, exercising, and eating more healthy. Well, just as we detox our bodies from time to time, we absolutely should detox our minds as well! We need to make sure that the things we are taking in from reading, music, social media, a busy lifestyle, and even people, are more beneficial than detrimental to our mental fitness. You may not even think anything of these things, but if your mind is in a weakened state you are more susceptible to becoming a pawn in the devil's grubby little hands. When your mind is unfit, the devil is able to find various ways to get in and have a field day adding additional chaos to your mind in the form of toxic thoughts, words, doubts, and fears, weakening your mind even more so that you end up a hot cluttered and confused mess! You need to guard your mind so that absolutely NO weapon that is formed against it can prosper!

Detoxing your mind is crucial to your well-being, but it can sometimes be painful. Letting go of family, friends, and old habits is difficult. We have to make the conscious decision to truly let go of the things keeping our mind unfit, and let God heal us. Jeremiah 29:11(KJV) says, "For I know the thoughts that I think toward you, saith the LORD, thoughts of peace, and not of evil..." The promises in God's Word are a balm to any part of our temple that is not fit. There is no other healing like it. So, although it can be painful, mind detox needs to be done so that your mind is 'fit' enough to discern, obey, and live God's will for you. It will also help you to focus fully on God, and His will for not just your temple fitness, but every aspect and area of your everyday life.

One way I have found helpful to detox my mind is by taking stock of whether or not I have allowed anything or anyone to take my focus off of God. I am a busy bee by nature. But, I have found that the busier I allow myself to become, the more likely I am to neglect my relationship with

God. Notice I said 'allow'. This means I have made a conscious decision and choice to be so busy that I become overwhelmed....unfocused on God, ready to pull my hair out, not sleeping, and becoming a shrew! When I allow myself to become too busy I start to neglect my prayer, devotion, and study time with God; forgetting just how much like food and air those things are to me. It is only when I have become so overwhelmed, frustrated, depressed, unhappy, and maybe a little bald, that I realize I have moved too far away from my Heavenly Father. God does not intend for us to be so 'busy' that we forget about Him. Untamed busyness is a tool of the devil, and when we allow ourselves to get so busy that we are no longer focused on God, we are no longer under the yoke of Jesus Christ, but the yoke of the devil...B.U.S.Y.=Being Under Satan's Yoke. This type of busyness is toxic to our entire temple, not just our mind. However, it will attack the mind first. We have to take measures to get rid of this type of busyness and the people, things, and situations that can poison the mind of our temple. But how do you eliminate busyness from your life so that your mind is fit and focused on the things of God?

Some things that I have found successful, and suggest for you, in helping me keep my mind fit and guarded from toxic busyness are:

1) Seek God's face, and ask His forgiveness for straying from His will. Ask Him to show you the things causing your mind to be unfit, and to guide you to remove those things. Give Him praise for not leaving or forsaking you. I do this through prayer and studying His Word, thus restoring my prayer, devotion, and study life.

2) Find scriptures and quotes or phrases that that speak life into your mind. Sometimes we are our own worst enemy, and the negative thoughts we think of ourselves, and the negative words we may say, like... "I am so fat", "I look like a slob", "I'm not smart enough'. These things can grow like fungus in your mind and you must be careful. Using God's Word to create positivity in your mind will help in keeping your mind toxin free.

3) Get a journal and for each day, for 30 days, make two columns. In the first column, list all the things, situations, and yes, people, you have allowed to clutter up and corrode your mind with toxic words, actions, etc., and take your focus from God. In the second column, list how and why these things came to clutter and toxify your mind.

4) Remove physical clutter from around you—in your home, your car, etc. Basically get your house in order man! When my house is dirty...dishes in the sink, laundry piling up, needing to dust...my mind starts to feel bogged down with 'mental' to-do lists. Take a deep breath, and write a 'visual' to-do list. Put your list somewhere you can see it and check off each task on the list as you complete it.

5) Make a prayer journal and start writing down prayers asking God to help you to remove busyness, people, and distractions that may be hindering you from keeping and maintaining a fit mind.

Doing all, or some, of these things helps me, and can help you, to regain focus and equip us to better recognize the things that we might be allowing to take us away from the will of our Heavenly Father. I give God thankful praise for always welcoming me back with open arms. His Word promises that He will 'never leave us or forsake us'; and that if we seek Him with our 'whole heart, He will be found'. And as always, I have found the promises of God's Word to be true.

I need you to understand that you don't detox your mind and get mind-fit and then bam! it's done and you will never be 'unfit' in your mind again. Oh-oh no, honey! I can't tell you the number of times I have had to detox my mind, but I can tell you I will probably have to do it many more times. Because the bottom line is that yes, we are fearfully and wonderfully made, but we definitely are not perfectly and flawlessly made! Sometimes we just become caught up in life in general. So think of a mind detox like this...say you make the decision to start eating healthier; you buy what's needed, follow a meal plan from a book or create your own, and you get started. But, you aren't just doing it for a day, right? You have made a conscious decision to make a change in your lifestyle and want to continue in that way. So, in detoxing your mind, remember you have to work at it and continue in that way by using the Word of God, and whatever other tools and insights He gives you in order to maintain and continue on in having a fit mind. I believe 1Chronicles 16:11(KJV) sums it up when it says: "Seek the Lord and his strength, seek his face continually". And that is the key...seeking God, and seeking him continually.

When detoxing your body you rely on *willpower* to help you continue with a maintaining healthier lifestyle. Well, you need to remember that it will be trusting in God after seeking Him, that will get you through detoxing your mind. Proverbs 3:5-6(KJV) tells us to "Trust in the Lord with all thine heart; and lean not unto thine own understanding. In all thy ways acknowledge him, and he shall direct thy paths".

God's plans for you are not to harm you, but to give you hope. So, seek God. Trust God. Hope in God. Allow Him in to heal and clear your mind. Allow God to help you become, and stay, mind-fit.

STUDY SCRIPTURES:

- Jeremiah 29:11 & 13
- 1 Chronicles 16:11
- Proverbs 3:5 & 6

JOURNALING QUESTIONS

1. What are some signs specific to you, that let you know that your mind is becoming 'unfit'? Do you allow yourself to be overtaken by these signs? If so, why?

_____

_____

_____

_____

_____

_____

2. When you see signs that you are becoming mindfully 'unfit', what steps do you take to overcome them? Do you seek God?

_____

_____

_____

_____

3. What people or things have, or are, causing you to have an 'unfit' mind?

_____

_____

_____

_____

4. What thoughts or words are you thinking or saying to yourself that may be causing your mind to be toxic or cluttered? What scriptures or inspirational phrases can you use to help you speak life into your mind?

_____

_____

_____

_____

5. What things do you do to detox your mind? Do they help you to place your focus back on God?

_____

_____

_____

_____

6. How do you differentiate between tamed and untamed busyness? Are you at risk of being B.U.S.Y.?

_____

_____

_____

_____

CHAPTER 3
JOURNEY LEG: BODY-FIT

Now that we have your mind cleared and fit, you probably want to tackle getting your body fit, right? It only makes sense. However, there are two sides to being body fit...physical and healing. The physical being weight loss, exercise, eating habits. The healing side has a focus on how to stay healthy, and not letting illness rule your life.

Being body fit is a mindset, and once you have a clear and fit mind, you are better able to make decisions on how to get body fit and maintain that fitness for your temple. In the physical, being body fit means just that...you are fit in your body by having and maintaining a healthy body weight, eating habits, and exercise program. However, it is important that first and foremost YOU are happy with your physical appearance.

In Chapter 1, we talked about loving yourself as God loves you. That also means seeing yourself as He sees you...fearfully and wonderfully made, and in His image. In the first chapter, I also reminded you that 'we are not our own'. Yes, God has blessed us with this temple; and although we are not our own, we are charged with being a good steward over this temple. That means maintaining a healthy lifestyle with good foods, exercise, rest, and remembering just how amazingly made we are.

It is important to have and keep a 'realistic' view of yourself and your body. Being a size 24 and wearing a size 18 is not healthy for your body or your body image; and I can't image that it is very comfortable at all! You must learn to accept how God has made you. To want to majorly change your body based on what people, media, and society is wrong, and in my opinion an affront to God. I admit that there was a time in my life when I wanted to look like the popular girls, girls in the magazines and on tv--fake hair, fake nails, tons of makeup, provocative and unflattering clothing. However, as I grew older I realized that because my 'mind' was unfit, I was seeking and portraying an unrealistic sense of self. I didn't really exist, and under all of that 'fakeness', was a little girl still trying to fit in. Take it from me, it's hard, and expensive, to keep up with a false sense of self; an unrealistic self. So, accepting, loving and seeing yourself as God does will help with keeping a realistic view of yourself.

Just like you have to have a realistic view of your physical appearance, you need to do the same when you set out to lose weight. Here are some steps to take that will help you.

1) First and foremost, seek God first!
2) Do not set unrealistic or unattainable goals. Doing this will only lead to frustration and can result in serious setbacks both physically and mentally.
3) Find or develop a reasonable course of action that will help you to reach your weight loss goals in a healthy manner.
4) Do your due diligence on any program you choose to follow. You want to choose the best program for you and your needs. Don't try to go with the latest and most popular weight loss fad because every program is not for every 'body'. Most of those clients already have a plan they want to use when they come to me; they just need the guidance and encouragement of someone outside of family and friends to help them reach their goal.
5) Do not pay a ton of money to lose weight. There are a lot of programs and groups that charge you for food, meetings, etc., and it all that can add up to hundreds

and sometimes thousands of dollars! As I mentioned, there are plenty of programs available; you just need to find the best one for you.

6) Get a group together of like-minded people who are also on a journey to better health and wellness. In my practice, I do a lot of group coaching for health and wellness, and honestly I have seen better results with my group clients compared to my individual clients.

The other part of the physical side of being body fit is….the dreaded exercise or workout. Exercise doesn't have to be the scary part of health and wellness that it has been portrayed to be. I am here to tell you, if you are willing to put in about 30-45 minutes a day, you will accelerate your weight loss, and feel better too! Most people think they have to work out for hours a day, seven days a week. This is so not true! Exercise is only 20% of your weight loss. And walking, just plain old walking, is the best exercise for shedding inches and pounds. I always suggest to my clients to start with a 30-minute walking regimen. Walking will help clear your mind, and prepare your body for more rigorous exercise such as cardio, when you are ready. Physical exercise can make you feel alive and more clear-headed. This is because you are activating and releasing that wonderful, happy little hormone called the endorphin.

Working out gives me a sense of accomplishment, and once I am in a routine I find my energy level is up, and my mood is much improved. I believe that physical exercise can also help with healing our bodies from sickness. I have also found that physical exercise helps my body continue healing after I have gotten over the flu or a cold. Walking helps relieve my headaches as well. When we exercise, we are more likely to rest better at night. It is so important to have not just a good nights' sleep, but a good nights' rest. Restful sleep is the time when our body is able to heal itself.

It is a terrible thing to be constantly ill or in pain. It impacts our quality of life, our relationships, our jobs, and can test our trusts and faith in God. We were created in such a way that our are meant to heal naturally. And exercise, a healthy diet, and a fit mind help to make this so. But it is a choice. We must choose to be healthy. You have to want to be healthy and healed. James 5:14-15 tells us that if we pray the prayer of faith, we will be healed; and God will restore us.

For over 20 years I was in constant and chronic pain. I was diagnosed with endometriosis in my early 20's, and chronic ovarian cyst syndrome in my mid 40's. There were times that I couldn't sit, I couldn't be on my feet or walk for long periods of time. And every time I went to the doctor they just gave me more pain meds, band-aids on the problem. In 2014 I decided enough was enough! I had just married my husband the year before and relocated to a new state. I had to find a new doctor, and I found a doctor who took the time to listen. I let her know that I know longer wanted to be sick and in pain. After my first appointment with her, I began praying the prayer of faith every single day, asking God to use this new doctor to help in healing my body. And the more I prayed that prayer of faith, the more God showed me that this doctor was going to be the one God used to heal me...and indeed she was. I ended having a much needed complete hysterectomy, and during my recuperation I made sure to get the rest I needed to help my body heal. I have been pain free going on three years. You see, I made a decision. I prayed my prayer of faith, I made sure to follow my doctor's orders and I 'rested' so that I could heal, and God answered. I prayed and spoke scriptures of healing into my body as I recuperated. And I prayed and spoke those scriptures with all the power, authority, and measure of faith that God has given me.

We have so much power when we pray and speak the Word of God into our physical being, and into our healing. Remember the faith that the woman with an issue of blood had? She knew without a doubt, and had faith without any doubt, that if she could just touch the hem of Jesus' cloak she would be healed....and she was. We must have that same faith. We must pray our prayer of faith so that God may heal and restore this amazing temple He has blessed us with.

STUDY SCRIPTURES:
- James 5:14-15
- Luke 8:43-48

JOURNALING QUESTIONS

1. What one thing do you want to change about your physical body, and why? Have you taken any steps to make the changes? If so, what are those change?

_____

_____

_____

_____

_____

2. What kind of fitness and/or weight loss plan(s) have you used in the past? Were you able to stick with it? If so, how? If not, why?

_____

_____

_____

_____

_____

3. Write a prayer of faith for any illness or pain you are currently experiencing.

_____

_____

_____

_____

CHAPTER 4

JOURNEY LEG: HEART-FIT

"Above all else, guard your heart....". What profound words from Proverbs 4:23(NIV). Several years ago, this scripture actually healed *my* heart.

I remember as clear as if it were yesterday; late July, 2011. I had just finished an interview for a job that I knew was not for me. I was sitting in my daughters car. It had to be at least 95 degrees outside and felt 150 degrees in the car, and her power windows were broken...if you rolled them down it was very difficult to roll them back up. So, there I am, sitting in a stifling car, just after an interview that left me even more discontent than I had already been feeling. And my heart hurt. I had been in a relationship that ended badly, and my heart just hurt. I remember sitting there in that hot car, finally letting the dam of tears break, and crying out to God, asking Him, "Why does my heart hurt so bad?". And I heard that still small voice say, 'Because you forgot to guard your heart with Me."

Our heart is fragile and does indeed need guarding. The only way to guard the heart is by staying in accord with God. Seeking His face, seeking Him wholeheartedly. Proverbs 3:5(NIV) tells us to "Trust in the Lord with all your heart..." When we trust God with all our heart, and allow Him to hold it and keep it safe, any heartache will be lessened; and we are more able to get through any sorrow and hurt that might come our way. You see, God wants us to come to Him when we are hurting, to trust Him and allow Him to comfort us. It is when we entrust our heart to people and things of the world that the pain of a broken heart can feel most unbearable.

Later that day, after I returned home from my interview, I immediately went to my room and got my Bible. I knelt by the side of my bed and asked God to show me through His Word how to guard my heart. I knew I had some scriptures highlighted, and sure enough Proverbs 4:23 was one of those verses. I prayed and spoke that scripture to my heart for weeks. And slowly, and lovingly, just as a surgeon may sometimes have to massage a heart back to beating, my Heavenly Father massaged my hurting heart to healing.

So how do we get to the point where our heart feels such pain? Well, as I mentioned before, we have to take care to guard our heart against people and things of the world.

Jeremiah 17:9(KJV) says "The heart *is* deceitful above all *things*; and desperately wicked: who can know it?" Who indeed?

Just as toxic people and things can poison our mind, those same things can do that to our heart. When we lean towards our own understanding, instead of trusting in God, we are more susceptible to being hurt because we are letting the emotions and feelings of our heart guide our thinking. We cannot manage our heart on our own, because without God we are emotional creatures. Our worldly heart beats off of emotion and we all know what kind of trouble emotions can get us into!!

The Amplified Bible expounds on Jeremiah 17:9 this way, "The heart is deceitful above all things, and it is exceedingly perverse and corrupt and severely, mortally sick!..." My goodness! It's a wonder we are able to make any decision clearly at all! But, just as deceitful as the heart can be, there is also joy in knowing that when our heart is guarded the way it should be, we are able to exude healthy and Godly emotions and feelings. Romans 10:10(AMP) says, "For with the heart a person believes (adheres to, trusts in, and relies on Christ)..."; and Romans 10:11(AMP) concludes that, "The Scripture says, No man who believes in Him [adheres to, relies on, and trusts in Him] will [ever] be put to shame *or* be disappointed." Glory to God! So, because we believe in

Him, because we rely on and trust in Him, we are free of the shame of being a victim of an unguarded heart. We cannot expect to avoid the pains of the heart unless we trust in Godly heart, and not our emotional heart. The heart is the 'ear' of our temple and is probably the most important part, along with the mind, of our temple. There is a peace in knowing that God has my heart guarded, and Philippians 4:7(KJV) says it well, "And the peace of God, which passeth all understanding, shall keep your hearts and minds through Christ Jesus." It is important to make sure that our mind and heart are both focused on God, and only God, and not people, things, world, or ourselves.

STUDY SCRIPTURES:

- Proverbs 4:23
- Proverbs 3:5
- Jeremiah 17:9
- Romans 10:10 & 11
- Philippians 4:7

JOURNALING QUESTIONS

1. Was there ever a time that you left your heart 'unguarded'? What was it and how did you get through it?

_____

_____

_____

_____

_____

2. When was a time that your heart felt like it breaking? What steps did you take to heal it?

_____

_____

_____

_____

3. In what ways to you allow God in so that He can guard your heart?

_____

_____

_____

_____

CHAPTER 5

JOURNEY LEG: SOUL-FIT

When I think about being soul fit, I think about taking rest in God. Taking rest in His majesty, taking rest in His Word, taking rest in His presence, and especially taking rest in His love. The soul is where we can find peace, as long as we look and find it in God. How wonderful is it to know that when our mind, body, heart and spirit are worn and tired, overwhelmed, disillusioned, we have our soul where we can take rest in the Lord.

Psalm 62:1(NIV) says "Truly my soul finds rest in God; my salvation comes from him." How awesome and comforting is that?! To know that no matter how hectic life gets, no matter how much pain or sorrow we feel, no matter how cluttered our mind, we can rest our soul in the safest place there is….God's hands. I know what it is to have a weary soul. To feel so overwhelmed you can't get a grasp on even the simple things. But then I remember I am not alone. I have

God to comfort and to hold me, and comfort me from the storms of life and the world.

When you truly find rest in God, your soul is filled with a peace that consumes your entire temple. The Amplified Bible says in Philippians 4:7, "And God's peace [shall be yours, that tranquil state of a soul assured of its salvation through Christ,...] which transcends all understanding shall garrison and mount guard over your hearts and minds in Christ Jesus." Your heart and mind, are guarded by the peace you receive from resting your soul in God, through our mighty Savior, Jesus the Christ!! So, in knowing God and resting our soul in Him, we will then know peace.

Sometimes your soul needs to be restored as it rests. Psalm 23:3(ESV) says, "He restores my soul...." I know with how full my schedule is as a wife, life coach, auxiliary president, writer, mother, grandmother...whew! I need some rest and restoration for my soul quite a bit. I find that I am best at peace and rest to restore my soul when I spend time with God, studying His Word. The scripture holds so much power! It holds comfort, healing, guidance, and love. We just have to make time to study and explore God's Word to find peace and rest for our soul. Jeremiah 29:13(KJV) says "And ye shall seek me, and find me, when you shall search for me with all your heart." It is up to you to seek God's face and seek the rest your soul needs. Yes, He is sees all and is aware of what we are going through, but He wants us to *seek* Him; to come to Him of our own accord. And although sometimes it is difficult but we still must do it.

Sometimes we get so caught up with everything, but we must make every effort to run to the comfort and peace of our Father's presence. For me, just knowing that when all else fails, when no one is there for me, I now my Lord hasn't left me or forsaken me. Sometimes, I feel His presence as a small tickle in the back of my mind, or a patter in my heart. Other times I feel as if He is sitting right next to me. Those things remind me that He is going to be waiting for me whenever I need Him. I take comfort and solace in that.

So, to become soul-fit you must seek God with all your heart, rest in Him, allow Him to rest in you, and use the scripture to speak peace and rest to your soul.

STUDY SCRIPTURES:

- Psalm 62:1
- Philippians 4:7
- Psalms 23:3
- Jeremiah 29:13

JOURNALING QUESTIONS

1. What things have caused you to have unrest in your soul? How did you deal with them?

_____

_____

_____

_____

_____

2. What are some scriptures that give you peace and rest in God?

_____

_____

_____

CHAPTER 6

FINAL DESTINATION: SPIRIT-FIT

Well, you have arrived! You have taken a journey to getting your spirit fit and just look at you!!! Your mind is detoxed and clear, your body is shimmering with new life and health, your heart is now guarded safely, and your soul is rested and restored. Wasn't it worth it??

Now, let's talk about what we can do to be spirit-fit. To be spiritually fit you have to accept Jesus Christ as your Lord and Savior, so that you may receive this great gift, a comforter, the Holy Spirit. One of the most amazing things about the spirit is that it is alive!! The Holy Spirit moves us to do the will of God and to carry out His direction. As our mind needs to be fit to make clear decisions, the spirit needs to be fit to receive directives from God. Our spirit can speak to God, and God can speak to our spirit. Our spirit can't be seen but it prays for us, and acts on our behalf. During times of trouble, sorrow, sickness, times when we just don't feel like praying, or at times when we don't feel that God is hearing us, it is a comfort to know that the Holy Spirit is working on our behalf. In Romans 8:26(AMP), we can see that this is true as it says, "So too the [Holy] Spirit comes to our aid *and* bears us up in our weakness; for we do not know what prayer to offer nor how to offer it worthily as we ought, but the Spirit Himself goes to meet our supplication and pleads in our behalf with unspeakable yearnings and groanings too deep for utterance." Wow!! How can you not find comfort in that!? How can you not see just how powerful the Holy Spirit living in you is? And that power lives in each and every one of us who has confessed a belief in Jesus the Christ!! I feel not just comfort, but also joy in knowing that when I am at my lowest, at my weakest or saddest, or sickest; when I don't feel I have the strength to get through, Jesus has provided a way for me to still communicate with my heavenly Father.

So many things come against us, trying to block the will of our God-given spirit. Fear, discouragement, anxiety; all of this can and will come against us by attacking our mind, body, heart, soul, *and* spirit. But God's Word tells us in 2nd Timothy 1:7(KJV) that "For God hath not given us the spirit of fear; but of power, and of love, and of a sound mind." Do you see that?? You not only have the spirit working on your behalf, but it has power. Power to change your situations, power to change your attitude. You have the power within you! As a child of God, you are equipped with the authority to use the power of the Holy Spirit, in combination with God's Word, to speak life into every area and situation of your life. Just knowing that Jesus sent such an ally for me gives me peace of mind and rest in my soul. But, we must be careful to be used by the spirit the way God wishes. And that is where the fruits of the spirit come in.

Love, joy, peace, patience, kindness, goodness, faithfulness, gentleness, self-control. These are the fruits of the spirit and they help to govern the parts of our temple.

1. **Love**. As we know love is many things. God is love and we are to walk in that love by showing it to others. We must give love to others even when we don't like them very much. In 1 Corinthians 13:4-7 we are told exactly what love is. Love endures long, is patient and kind, does not envy, does not boast, and is not proud. Love is not rude, unbecoming, or self-seeking. Love bears all things, believes all things, hopes all things, and endures all things. This is what God's love should look like in us. God's love should shine through us as brightly and warming as the sun.

2. **Joy**. When you have the joy of God in you there is no

better feeling. I am reminded of a Sunday school song, "I've got the joy, joy, joy, joy, down in my heart....". That song always lightens my mood even now as an adult. Even through dark times, times when I can't see a way through, I find comfort in knowing that on the other side there will be joy because God brought me through.

3. **Peace**. This word brings a sigh from me. But it also sometimes brings a longing to have this very thing called peace. Believing and trusting in God should bring you perfect peace and comfort. Romans 15:13(KJV) says, "Now the God of hope fill you with all joy and peace in believing, that ye may abound in hope, through the power of the Holy Ghost." See there? Once again the power of the Holy Spirit is shown here, in a way to bring us peace.

4. **Patience**. Many of us struggle with this particular spiritual fruit. We live in a society of now, now, now, and hurry, hurry, hurry. We want everything done today and right this minute, and in doing so we become angry and frustrated. But Ecclesiastes 7:9 tells us to "Be not quick in your spirit to become angry..." We must remember to keep our focus on God, from whence our help comes.

5. **Kindness**. We must strive to be kind, even when we don't want to be. We must offer it as a gift. Many times we allow others who are unkind to us, to affect our

treatment of them. But, we must always try to look past another person's lack of kindness and shower them with my own. My thought is that I don't know what that unkind person may be going through, and that might be what is making them unkind. Proverbs 3:3(AMP) instructs us to "Let not mercy and kindness [shutting out all hatred and selfishness] and truth [shutting out all deliberate hypocrisy or falsehood] forsake you;..." When you are kind, you are a blessing to others; and you will be blessed in return.

6. **Goodness**. We know about the goodness of God. And because we know, we should be an example of His goodness; especially since He has been so good to us. In Galatians 6:10(NIV) we find that when we have the opportunity we should do good to all people. I see this as another opportunity to bless others, as God has and continues to bless us.

7. **Faithfulness**. How wonderful is God's grace that through that grace we are able to receive this wonderful gift of the spirit? I love the scripture Matthew 25:23(KJV), "....Well done, good and faithful servant; thou hast been faithful over a few things, I will make thee ruler over many things..." Faithfulness is also obedience. Obedience to God's ways and His direction for your life.

8. **Gentleness**. We must not only be kind to others, but gentle in our words, actions, and treatment of others. Treat others with the same gentleness that God shows you. Proverbs 15:1 reminds us that "A gentle answer turns away wrath, But a harsh word stirs up anger.". Remember, there is both life and death in the tongue.

9. **Self-Control**. We must be careful not to rush into anything, especially that which is not of God. And if we are guided to something by the spirit, then we must remember what Proverbs 25:28(KJV) says, "He that hath no rule over his own spirit is like a city that is broken down, and without walls." I don't know about you, but I absolutely do not like going about doing things all willy-nilly and of my own accord. I have a constant prayer running through my mind asking God to help me to be able to discern His direction and will, so that I am able to do what is right and pleasing in His sight.

I love how the Amplified Bible asks us in 1 Corinthians 7:19 that, "Do you not know that your body is the temple (the very sanctuary) of the Holy Spirit Who lives in you, Whom you have received [as a Gift] from God?...." The Holy Spirit dwells in you; waiting to work in and through you as God sees fit. Just as fruit trees and plants have to be cared for, pruned, soil fit for growing, you must also tend to the parts of your temple so that you are able to allow the Holy Spirit to use and guide you so that you are able to bear good spiritual fruit.

STUDY SCRIPTURES:

- Romans 8:26
- 2 Timothy 1:17
- 1 Corinthians 13:4-7
- Romans 15:13
- Ecclesiastes 7:9
- Proverbs 3:3
- Galatians 6:10
- Matthew 25:23
- Proverbs 15:1
- Proverbs 25:28

JOURNALING QUESTIONS

1. When was the first time that you felt you were being led by the Holy Spirit?

   _____

   _____

   _____

   _____

2. How do you know when and if you are being led by the Holy Spirit?

   _____

   _____

   _____

   _____

3. Which fruit(s) of the spirit do you find the hardest to grow in the soil of your temple? Which one do you produce the most fruit with?

_____

_____

_____

_____

CHAPTER 7

MAINTAINING YOUR SPIRITUAL FITNESS

I am so excited for you! You made the choice to take this journey and you are to be commended for it! I hope that you have arrived to the end of this journey better off than when you started, and that you are now better equipped to maintain not just your spiritual fitness, but overall temple fitness.

So....now what? How do you continue on a daily journey to being temple-fit and maintaining your spiritual fitness?

First, get a journal. Journals are a great way to detox your mind. Writing can help release the chaos in your mind. I use journals to write daily to-do lists, keep track of prayer requests, and to unburden my mind and heart. Once you get a journal, you can also go back through the chapters of this book and write down all of the scriptures. Use the scriptures to make a study plan to use in your prayer or devotional time.

Second, continue to seek God with all your heart. Study His Word diligently, remember to trust in Him and not your own understanding. Remember, you have the Holy Spirit and its power to help guide you, and act on your behalf.

Third, study the answers you gave to the journaling questions at the end of each chapter in this book. One thing I do personally, and have my clients do, is to go back a month or so later and see if any of the answers might be different than where you are presently. It is a fun exercise and helps you to see the progress, or lack of progress, you are making in maintaining you temple and your spiritual fitness.

We must have a fit mind, body, heart, and soul, so that our spirit is able to do the will of God through us. You can't fully do the will of God if your mind is bogged down in chaos, your body is sick or unhealthy, your heart is not guarded against the attack of the enemy, and your soul not rested, refreshed, and restored. If you are going to do the will of God, you need to be fit in mind, body, heart, and soul, so that the spirit dwelling in you can do its part to contribute in keeping you temple-fit.

I hope you have enjoyed this journey as much as I have. I want to leave you with this: Understanding your temple, and how it works, is the first step to creating and maintaining a fit temple. Always remember that all parts of your temple need to be given attention to maintain their individual fitness. Romans 8:28(KJV) is a perfect reminder of this, "And we know that all *things* work together for good to them that love God..." You need look no further than the Word of God to understand your God-given temple and how to care for and maintain it. You see, God's Word provides us with all of the tools, power, and authority to have and maintain a fit temple, and as you study God's Word you will become more attuned to how to take care of it....God's way.

STUDY SCRIPTURE:

- Romans 8:28

JOURNALING QUESTIONS

1. What part of your temple needs the most attention? How will you go about becoming temple-fit in that part?

_____

_____

_____

_____

2. If you could change any part of your temple, which part would you change? Why?

_____

_____

_____

3. Write a prayer of faith about maintaining your mind-fitness.

_____

_____

_____

_____

4. Write a prayer of faith about maintaining your body-fitness.

_____

_____

_____

_____

5. Write a prayer of faith about maintaining your heart-fitness.

_____

_____

_____

_____

6. Write a prayer of faith about maintaining your soul-fitness.

_____

_____

_____

_____

7. Write a prayer of faith about maintaining your spiritual-fitness.

_____

_____

_____

_____

ABOUT THE AUTHOR

Camielle L. Moore is an author, inspirational speaker, Christian Life Coach, and the founder of Temple-Fit Ministries-Christian Life, Health & Wellness Coaching. She is passionate about being Temple-fit for not just ourselves, but for the kingdom of God. Camielle believes and teaches that when we are temple-fit in mind, body, heart, soul, and spirit, we are better equipped and able to be Christian-fit in all areas of our life.

Camielle would love to hear from you! You can reach her at camielle@templefitlifecoaching.com

ACKNOWLEDGMENTS

I would like to first and foremost give thanks, praise, honor and glory to God, the head and light of my life.

To my Temple-Fit administrative director and partner, Tara Crumbie. Thank you for not just sharing, but also seeing my 'vision and calling' for this ministry. It was a wonderful and blessed day when God placed you in my life. Having you as a partner gives me the peace of mind and confidence to 'Live Into' my passion, and the purpose God has called me to. There are no words that will have express how much appreciate you…thank you!

To my children Richard, Rick, Alexandrea, Jaleesa, and Casey, thank you for being my heroes. For loving me despite all of the 'mom' moments I have put you through. For allowing me to minister to you even when you don't really want to hear it. God blessing me to be your mother is one of the greatest gifts I could have ever been blessed with.

To my grandbabies Ellianna, Nathanial, Xavier, Azaria, Quentin, Xevin, and Malyah, thank you for keeping me young.

To my mommy, Wanda, who always taught me to let nothing hold me back from living my life…no matter what anyone says; To my mama-in-law Thelma Moore who is always excited about anything I have going on.

I have saved the best for last…I would like to acknowledge the support and love of my MVP, my king, my husband, Terrance E. Moore. Thank you for your love and support as I worked to become temple-fit; and for reminding me to live Proverbs 3:5-6 as I travel my own journey to spiritual fitness. Thank you for respecting and encouraging God's call on my life, and helping me to walk in it.

www.ingramcontent.com/pod-product-compliance
Lightning Source LLC
LaVergne TN
LVHW051201080426
835508LV00021B/2737